CRIME SOLVERS

KILLER EVIDENCE

BE A POLICE DETECTIVE

by Alix Wood

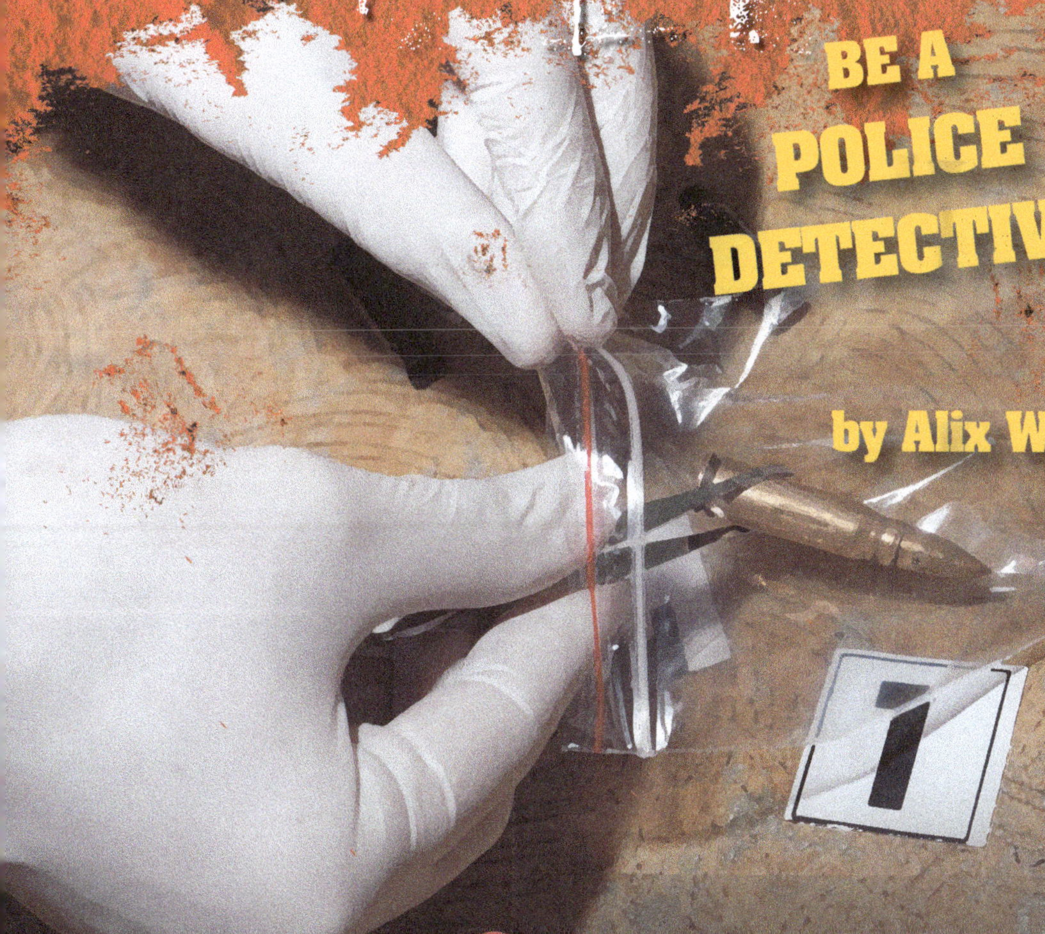

Gareth Stevens
PUBLISHING

Please visit our website, **www.garethstevens.com**. For a free color catalog of all our high-quality books, call toll free 1-800-542-2595 or fax 1-877-542-2596

Cataloging-in-Publication Data

Names: Wood, Alix.
Title: Killer evidence: be a police detective / Alix Wood.
Description: New York : Gareth Stevens Publishing, 2018. | Series: Crime solvers | Includes index.
Identifiers: ISBN 9781538206386 (pbk.) | ISBN 9781538206324 (library bound) | ISBN 9781538206201 (6 pack)
Subjects: LCSH: Criminal investigation--Juvenile literature. | Detectives--Juvenile literature.
Classification: LCC HV8073.8 W66 2018 | DDC 363.25028'4--dc23

First Edition

Published in 2018 by
Gareth Stevens Publishing
111 East 14th Street, Suite 349
New York, NY 10003

Produced for Gareth Stevens by Alix Wood Books
Designed by Alix Wood
Editor: Eloise Macgregor
Consultant: Stacey Deville, MFS, Texas Forensic Investigative Consultants

Photo credits: Cover, 1, 4-5, 6, 7, 8, 9 top, 11, 14, 15, 16, 20, 21, 24, 25, 26, 27, 28, 29, 33, 34, 35, 36, 38, 39, 40, 42, 43 © Adobe Stock Images, 9 bottom © Harvey Price, 10, 12, 13, 19 bottom, 22, 30, 31, 41 © Alix Wood, 37 © Thinkstock, all other images are in the public domain

Printed in the United States of America
CPSIA compliance information: Batch #CS17GS For further information contact Gareth Stevens, New York, New York at 1-800-542-2595.

CONTENTS

Call the Detective...

It's an April afternoon, and Phil Alton is walking along the street with his girlfriend, Sammy Healey. They are tired after working a long shift at the restaurant they run in Walters Valley. As they get near their house, they notice a dark car moving slowly toward them. The car window rolls down. Perhaps the driver needs directions? A man's arm reaches out. He's holding a gun...

DISPATCHER: Emergency 911. What is the location of your emergency?

SAMMY: I'm at Howard Avenue, Walters Valley.

DISPATCHER: What is your emergency, caller?

SAMMY: Help me. My boyfriend has been shot. He's badly hurt.

DISPATCHER: What is your name, caller?

SAMMY: Sammy Healey.

DISPATCHER: Police and an ambulance are on their way, Sammy. Stay on the line and we'll try to help you...

Date: April 22, 2017

Unit Number: 360

Reporting Officer's Notes

5:07 pm: Dispatch received a 911 call about a shooting at Walters Valley. The caller was the victim's girlfriend, Sammy Healey.

Unit 360 was **dispatched** and arrived at the scene at 5:19 pm. The officers found the victim had a gunshot wound to the neck. He was in critical condition. Officers gave first aid and asked for medical assistance.

5:22 pm: An ambulance arrived and the victim was rushed to John Walter Memorial Hospital. His girlfriend went with him in the ambulance. Officers taped off the **crime scene** to protect any evidence.

5:25 pm: Officers call in suggesting a detective may want to come and look at the crime scene. The victim is in a critical condition. It was a serious crime. Detective Olivier is on her way.

Case File

Solve It!

Police officers protect lives and property and enforce laws. Detectives investigate serious crimes by gathering facts and collecting evidence. Which of the tasks below would a detective do?

a) respond to an emergency call

b) patrol an area

c) interview a **suspect**

Answers on page 45

Meet a Detective

Hannah is reading through some case notes at the police station when the call comes through. She was just about to head off home. Now she is heading in the opposite direction, to Howard Avenue and the crime scene. She grabs an apple from her desk. It may be a while before she gets anything else to eat tonight.

Solve It!

Police detectives don't usually wear a police uniform. Why do you think that is?

a) because detectives aren't actually part of the police force.

b) because detectives are too important.

c) because detectives often need to be undercover. That means they don't want people to know they are police officers.

Answers on page 45

Name: **Hannah Olivier**

Job: Police detective

Education: High School Diploma, graduated from the Police Training Academy

Career: Was a police officer for two years and then moved to the Organized Crime Control Bureau. Became a Detective and moved to the Criminal Investigation Unit.

Favorite school subjects: English and Math.

Favorite part of her job: "It's great to get a call from the courts to say the **jury** just convicted your suspect. When you worked on that case, that makes the whole job worthwhile."

Worst part of her job: Being the detective on call and getting a call in the middle of the night after a long day.

Most interesting case: Hannah worked on a case where a woman had been murdered in her home. Her husband had been away at the time and had an airplane ticket to prove it. Hannah was suspicious, though, as he had just **insured** his wife for a large sum of money. It turned out that the husband had paid someone who looked like him to travel instead of him, using his ticket. With a perfect **alibi**, the husband had then murdered his wife.

Personnel File

Searching for Evidence

The ambulance has taken the victim to the hospital by the time Hannah gets to the scene. She looks at the evidence she has to work with. **Witnesses** saw the gun used in the crime being thrown out of the car window, along with an old piece of cloth. Bullet casings were scattered on the street. This could all be useful evidence.

Guns and Gangs

Gangs sometimes carry out **drive-by** shootings. Someone will fire a weapon from a car and then speed away. Often, the car has been stolen, so it is difficult to trace it to who committed the crime.

Hannah is hopeful she can find the criminal in this case. She has some evidence to work with. The first police officers at the scene did a great job. They found and marked every piece of evidence with numbered markers. Once everything is photographed, crime scene investigators will carefully bag everything up to take back to the station.

Top Tip

When detectives photograph evidence, these markers help identify each item clearly.

Hannah is hopeful of finding the criminal in this case. She has some evidence to work on. The first police officers at the scene had done a great job. They found and marked any piece of evidence using numbered markers. Once everything is photographed, crime scene investigators will carefully bag everything up to take back to the station.

Solve It!

What possible evidence could be found from the piece of old cloth?

a) the criminal's sweat or blood could possibly be found on the cloth, containing valuable **DNA** evidence

b) no evidence could be found on an old piece of cloth

Answers on page 45

SCIENCE DETECTIVE

Clues in the Spatter

Detectives can find useful clues in unlikely places. Experts can examine blood spatter at a scene and tell the detective what type of weapon was used, and how many times the victim was hit. They can tell if the attacker was right- or left-handed. They can work out the position of the victim, if the body was moved, and how long ago the crime was committed. All this from a few spatters of blood! How?

Blood Spatter

Blood is mainly made of water, so it behaves like water when it spatters. It is a little stickier though, and forms into round balls as it travels through the air. The size and shape of a blood spatter tells detectives quite a bit about how the person lost the blood.

Low-**velocity** blood drops

Occurs when a victim is injured and dripping blood.

Medium-velocity spatter

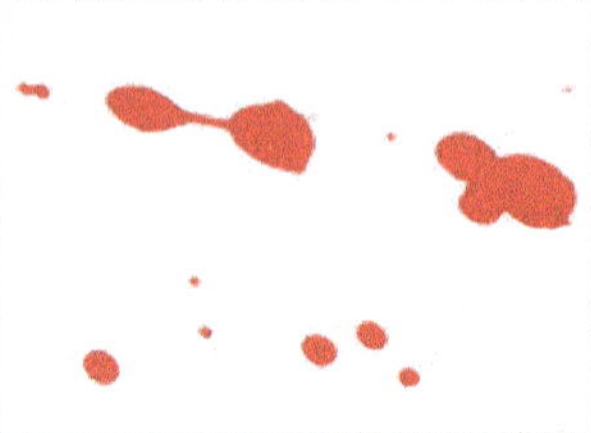

Happens after an attack with a blunt object, or a stabbing.

High-velocity spatter

Occurs with gunshot wounds. The droplets look like a fine spray.

EVIDENCE BAG CHALLENGE

Examine how different weapons create different blood spatter with this experiment. This is messy! Ask permission and wear old clothes, as the food dye WILL stain.

You will need: some large sheets of paper, strong tape, a sponge, hammer, baseball bat, screwdriver, some stage blood

Top Tip

If you don't have stage blood, mix 1.5 oz (44 g) cornstarch with 4.5 tablespoons of water. Mix in ⅓ pint (160 ml) of corn syrup. Add 2-3 teaspoons of red food color and 2 drops of green food color.

1. Tape the paper on an outside wall, covering a really large area. Cover the ground with paper, too. Put rocks around to hold the paper still.
2. Make your fake blood. Save some of the blood for another experiment on page 13. Cover its container in plastic wrap so that it doesn't dry out.
3. Pour two tablespoons of blood onto a damp sponge. Lay the sponge on the floor about arm's length from the wall. Strike the sponge with the hammer. Fake blood should spatter onto your paper. The droplets' tails should point toward the sponge.

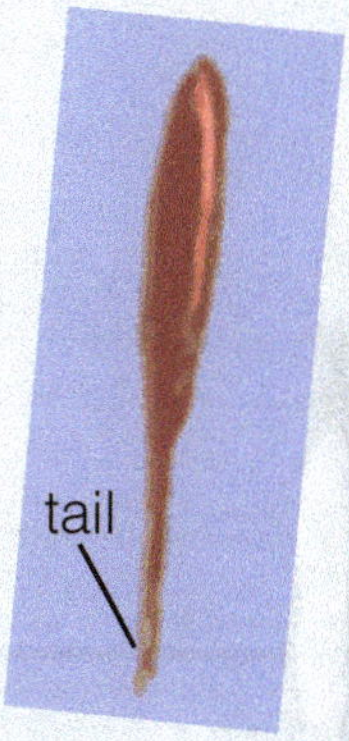

4. Replace the paper. Repeat the experiment, but this time strike the sponge with the baseball bat. Then replace the paper and repeat the experiment again by stabbing the screwdriver point into the sponge.

What differences do you notice between your "weapons"? Do the tails point toward where the sponge was? Try placing the sponge at different distances from the wall. What happens to the shapes of your spatters?

Examining the Scene

Hannah talks to some witnesses, and then goes over to look at the blood spatter left at the scene. The tails all point in the same direction. It is exactly where the witnesses say the car was when the shooting occurred. Hannah is fairly confident that her blood experts will tell her the gunman fired from the car.

From blood spatter, Hannah can tell if the victim was standing, sitting, or lying down when they were shot. The lower the **angle** that blood strikes a surface, the thinner and longer the bloodstain.

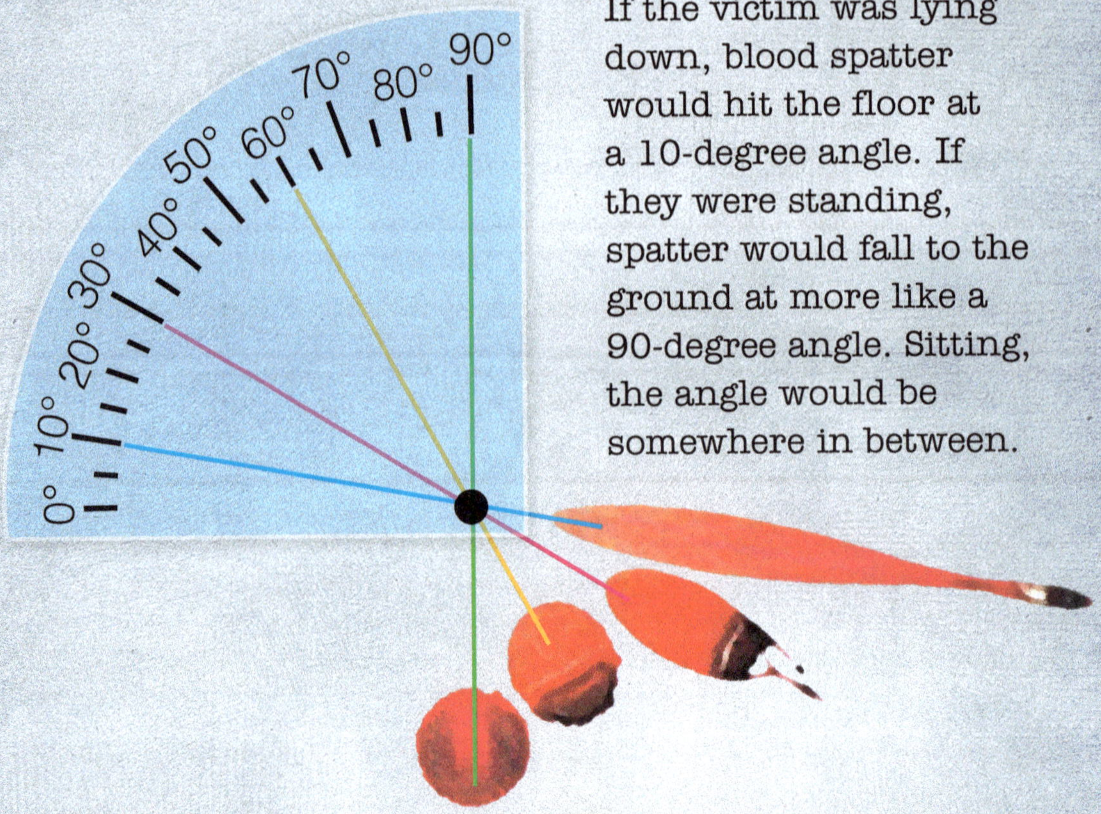

If the victim was lying down, blood spatter would hit the floor at a 10-degree angle. If they were standing, spatter would fall to the ground at more like a 90-degree angle. Sitting, the angle would be somewhere in between.

EVIDENCE BAG CHALLENGE

Using your leftover fake blood from page 11, try this challenge to see how the angle affects the shape of a bloodstain. Cover an area with several layers of newspaper before you start, and wear old clothes. The fake blood will stain.

You will need: a dropper, old newspapers, some card stock, fake blood.

1. Fill the dropper with the fake blood.
2. It is difficult to spatter blood at different angles, so to recreate the same effect, hold the card stock at different angles instead. First, to recreate someone lying down, hold the card stock at a steep angle. Release a drop of fake blood and look at the shape it makes.
3. Next, hold the card stock at a slightly flatter angle and repeat on a clean area. Is the shape different? Keep making the angle even flatter and record your findings.

Solve It!

A woman telephones police to say her husband has been beaten and kidnapped. You arrive at the warm house and see wet bloodstains on the floor. His wife tells you her husband was taken three hours ago. She has only just managed to untie herself to call the police. Do you believe her?

a) No, bloodstains in a warm house would most likely dry after 15 minutes. She's lying.

b) Yes, poor woman, why wouldn't you believe her?

Answers on page 45

Guns and Bullets

The Crime Scene Investigators are busy photographing and bagging up the evidence. Hannah takes a look at the gun as they carefully pack it away. It is the type of weapon often used by local gangs. The gunman has tried to wipe it clean, but it looks as if there may still be some fingerprints.

It is important for CSIs to record exactly where each bullet was found. They also must collect them to be examined. Sometimes, if bullets are found lodged in a wall, CSIs will even cut the piece of wall out to bring it back to the lab!

Top Tip

Bullets are stamped with a serial number. This can show where they were bought from, and even who bought them!

Experts who study guns and bullets are called **ballistic** experts. Investigators can tell a lot from a fired bullet. Guns often have unique marks inside the gun barrel that will scratch the casing as the bullet is fired. By studying the bullets, experts can sometimes match a bullet to a particular gun. They can also link crimes that may have been committed using the same gun, by checking police **databases**.

distinctive marks on a fired bullet

EVIDENCE BAG CHALLENGE

Ballistics experts can work out where a gun was fired from by studying bullet holes. Usually it is necessary for the bullet to have traveled through two objects to get a clear idea of the direction it came from. Try this experiment.

You will need: an empty cereal box, a meat skewer, an adult to help you, three pieces of paper numbered 1, 2, and 3.

1. Place the cereal box on a table. Position the three numbered labels to the left, middle, and right of the cereal box. Ask the adult to stand at one of the three positions and stab the skewer right through the cereal box, and then remove it. Leave the room until they are done.

2. Now try to work out where the adult was standing when they "attacked" the box. Was it position 1, 2, or 3?

Clue: Look through the first hole and move your head until you can see the far hole. What position are you in to do that?

SCIENCE DETECTIVE

The Art of Detecting

A good detective has to have a number of different skills. They must be skilled in the art of **reasoning**. They need an eye for detail, and a sharp memory, too. They must be able to keep an open mind, in case a lead they are following turns out to be wrong. Could you be a detective?

Using Reasoning

Reasoning is thinking about something in a **logical**, sensible way. Detectives use logic to work out problems during a case.

Your friend arrives at your house with wet hair. You might therefore believe that it is raining outside. A true detective must also think about other logical possibilities. Could your friend have just had a shower before coming out? Or have walked under a garden sprinkler? A detective must not leap to the easiest conclusion, but must keep an open mind.

Sharpen your observation skills by playing this game with a friend. Take turns being the detective. Pick a room in your home where there are quite a few easily removable items. Both of you should take time to look around the room and try to remember what is in it. Ask your friend to leave the room, and while they are gone, hide something. When your friend comes back in, they must figure out what is missing. If it is too hard, you can give them clues.

Can you find what has disappeared in picture B?

Top Tip

Try looking at the picture in a logical order. Start in the top left corner, then work to the right, then down.

Invisible Evidence

Back at her office, Hannah checks through her notes from the crime scene. She needs to send certain items away for expert tests. She sends the cloth found at the crime scene to be tested for any possible DNA evidence. The gunman used the cloth to wipe the gun clean of fingerprints. In getting rid of one kind of evidence, he may have accidentally left another!

Hannah hopes so. Traces of sweat on the cloth may give detectives a DNA profile. Everyone's DNA is different, so the results could be a vital clue that helps catch the gunman. It will take some time to get the results back. Hannah will have to wait a few weeks for an answer.

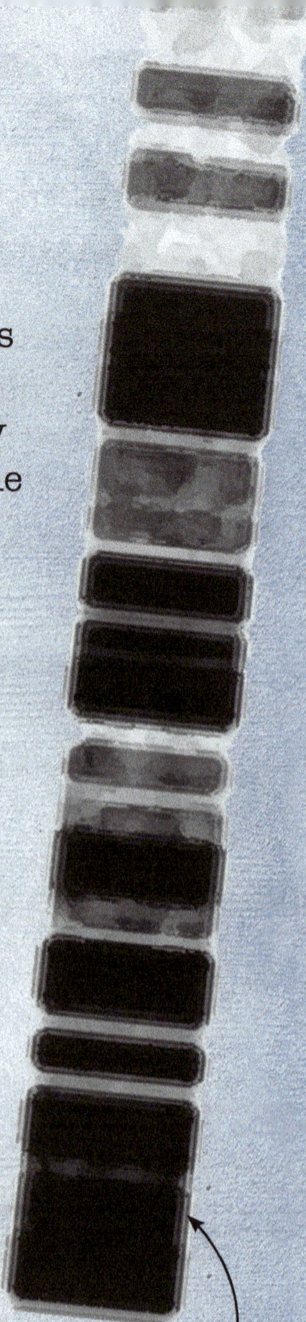

a strip of DNA code

Solve It!

Actually, not everyone's DNA is different. DNA is a product of our genes – the building blocks Inherited from our parents that make us each an individual. Can you think of a group of people who might have identical DNA?

a) anyone from the same family

b) identical twins

c) people that were born in the same area

Answers on page 45

Fingerprint experts check the gun for any traces of a print. Most of the gun had been wiped clean, but they did find what is known as a **partial** print. Half a print is better than nothing.

Anyone arrested for a crime usually has their fingerprints and DNA samples taken and put on a police database. Then, police can search the database for a match when either are found at a crime scene. They'll run the partial print through the database and see if it comes up with a match.

Types of Fingerprint

Fingertips have slightly raised lines that form patterns, and every finger has its own unique pattern. Look at your fingertips under a magnifying glass. Can you see one of these typical fingerprint patterns? Most people have loop patterns. The next most common pattern is the whorl. The rarest fingerprint is an arch.

loop whorl arch

Press your finger into an ink pad, or gently cover it in marker. Press your finger onto a **deflated** balloon. Wait for it to dry. Then blow up the balloon a little until you can see your fingerprint in detail.

Finding Some Leads

After searching the ballistics databases, Hannah's team discovers that marks on the bullets found at the scene matched some from a shooting that happened a year ago. They must have been fired by the same gun. The gunman in that case is now in jail. Hannah arranges to go and interview the man in jail. Interviewing people is one of the main parts of a detective's job.

Top Tip

Some people don't want to talk to the police, especially if they are afraid they will be connected to a crime. Detectives have to think of ways that might persuade the people they interview to talk.

First, the team reviews the previous shooting to try to find a link. Meanwhile, news comes in that Phil Alton is recovering in the hospital. Perhaps Hannah will soon get a chance to interview him, too.

Interviewing

Detectives use a variety of methods to interview people. A witness or victim will generally be telling the truth, but may struggle to remember details. A detective needs to help them try to remember exactly what happened. They often use a method known as the Cognitive Interview Method. The detective tries to get the interviewee to recreate the event in their head, to jog their memory. The interviewees are encouraged to express their emotions. This helps them relive the event, which may mean they will be able to recall more small details.

A suspect may lie or be unwilling to talk. These interviews need to be carefully handled. Detectives use a number of techniques. They sometimes play "good cop, bad cop." One of them seems friendly, while the other asks hard questions. The suspect may confess to the good cop, hoping they'll protect them from the bad cop! Sometimes detectives say they understand why the suspect may have committed the crime, hoping that they will encourage them to **confess**.

SCIENCE DETECTIVE

Getting the Right Answers

When questioned about a crime, most criminals will lie and say "I didn't do it." Confusingly, most **innocent** people will also say "I didn't do it" — because they didn't! How do you know when someone is telling the truth?

EVIDENCE BAG CHALLENGE

Try this memory challenge on a friend.
You will need: a pen and paper, a friend

1. Write a list of ten random words. Read them out loud to your friend. Ask them to repeat them in order back to you. How well did they do? Did they remember all the words in the right order?

2. Now, write down ten different words and read them out to your friend. This time ask them to repeat them back to you in reverse order, starting with the last word you said first. How well did they do?

It is usually much harder to remember things backward. The same is true of lies. Interviewers will sometimes ask a suspect to tell them what happened in reverse order. They often get muddled, and can be more easily caught in a lie.

Lying is harder to do than telling the truth. When you lie, you have to think on your feet, rather than just remember things. Detectives know this and can use this information to catch a liar. Try the experiment below and see if you can catch a liar.

Detective Skills

Ask a friend to tell you about a real event that has happened to them, and also think up an event that didn't really happen. Tell them to add lots of interesting details to both stories. In the real story, all the details must be true.

You must play detective and ask questions about both stories. Write down the questions and answers, or record your "interview" so you can check the facts. Say your friend's two stories are "I went to the zoo last week" and "My dad bought me a puppy." How are you going to tell which story is true? The trick is in the details.

Ask your friend lots of detailed questions about both stories. Ask how they got to the zoo, how long did the journey take, what animals did they see, what did they eat, who was with them, what did they wear? Watch to see if they **hesitate** before answering. Then try to trip them up by asking them the same questions again. Do they give you the same answers? Can you work out which story was a lie?

A Gangland Link?

Hannah heads to the county jail to interview Harry Cavallaro. He is the man who used the same gun that shot Phil Alton. She wants to know what happened to the gun, to give her a clue about who shot Alton.

Harry isn't in a very talkative mood. Hannah finds herself asking the same question over and over. "What happened to the gun?" Harry says it was stolen from his car. He says he didn't report it missing because he didn't have a license for it. Hannah tries again. "What really happened to the gun?

Top Tip

Detectives try to ask questions that need a long answer, not just yes or no. They use phrases like "tell me," "explain to me," and "describe to me." These work better than phrases like "did you?"

Making Life Uncomfortable

A prison would be an uncomfortable setting for a police interview. When detectives interview a suspect at a police station, they try to make the interview room as uncomfortable as possible. If the suspect wants to get the process over with, then they are more likely to confess. The suspect is taken to a bleak room. They are given an uncomfortable chair and trapped in the corner of the room, next to a one-way mirror.

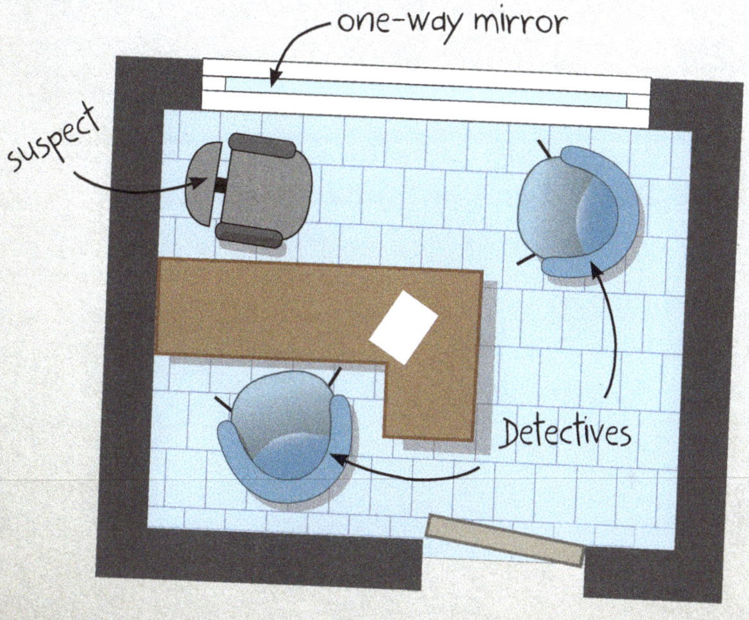

Solve It!

A family's DNA is very similar. The DNA results from the piece of cloth arrive. The DNA is almost identical to Harry Cavallaro's. But Harry was in prison when the shooting happened. What might that mean?

a) the DNA test results are wrong

b) The gunman must be related to Harry Cavallaro

Answers on page 45

Going Undercover

It looks as if the DNA result means that a member of the Cavallaro family was involved in the shooting. The family are the leaders of a crime gang. The police have been watching them for a long time. Some detectives have even been watching them undercover.

Have you ever dressed up as someone else? Perhaps you have dressed up as a zombie at Halloween? Imagine actually trying to live undercover for months, maybe years, as a real zombie. That would not be easy! How long do you think you would last before you got found out?

Top Tip

Looking the part is only half the battle. To be successful undercover you have to truly believe you are the role you are playing. Otherwise, you might get found out.

EVIDENCE BAG CHALLENGE

Do you think you could become another person? Try this game to find out! You and your friends will each create a disguise. Follow these steps to create a sneaky character!

You will need: dress-up clothes, some friends to make disguises, one friend to act as a judge

1. Create a backstory for your new identity. What is their name? Where are they from? Do they have a family? Making a character close to your age works the best.

2. Give your character a personality and unique qualities. Are they funny or shy? Polite or rude? Do they have an accent?

3. Find clothes for your new character that are very different from your usual wardrobe. Try a thrift store, or swap clothes with your friends. What clothes go with your character's personality?

4. Learn how to walk in your character's shoes! What is their posture like and how do they move? Watch television or a movie without the sound on. How do the different characters show their personalities with body language?

5. Each disguised person will have a conversation with the judge. Stay "in character" the whole time! The judge decides who has the most convincing disguise.

The Cavallaros

Detective work often involves spending hours searching through records and databases. Hannah's team finds out that Harry Cavallaro has three brothers. All three have police records. They search the files and pull out their fingerprints. Can detectives find a match with the print on the gun?

Hannah also asks the DNA experts to see if any of the brother's DNA might match the sample found on the piece of cloth. This case is moving forward!

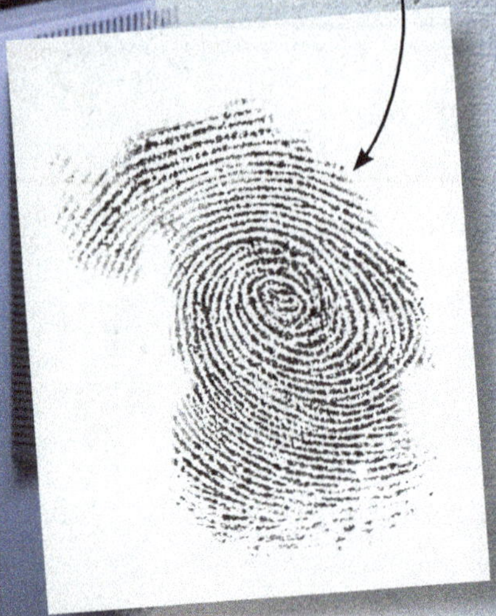

fingerprint found on gun

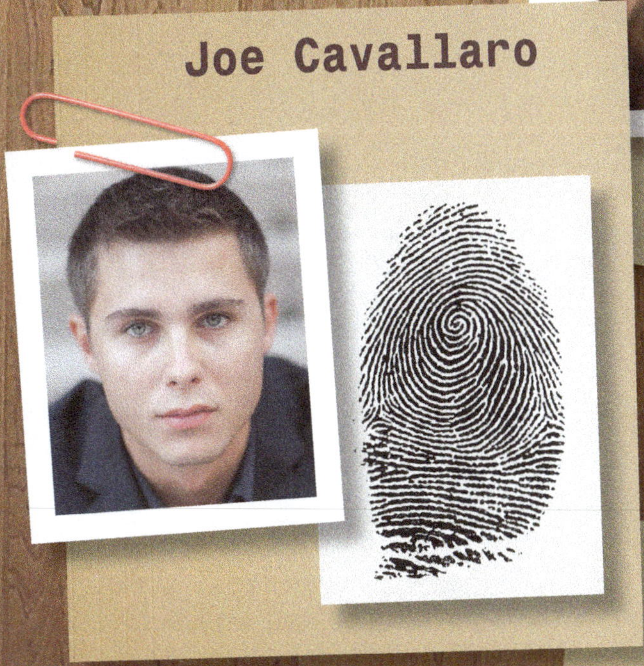

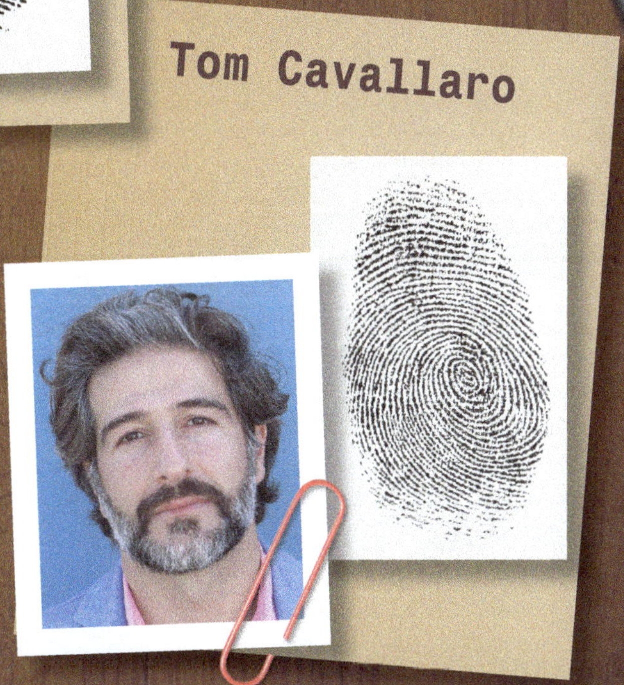

Solve It!

Whose fingerprints are a match to the partial print found on the gun?

a) Joe Cavallaro's

b) Mark Cavallaro's

c) Tom Cavallaro's

Answers on page 45

SCIENCE DETECTIVE

Be a Detective

Do you think you could be a good detective? Hannah's team has dug up the victim's phone records, bank statements, and appointment book. Look at Phil Alton's personal records below. Can you find any connection between Phil and the gunman?

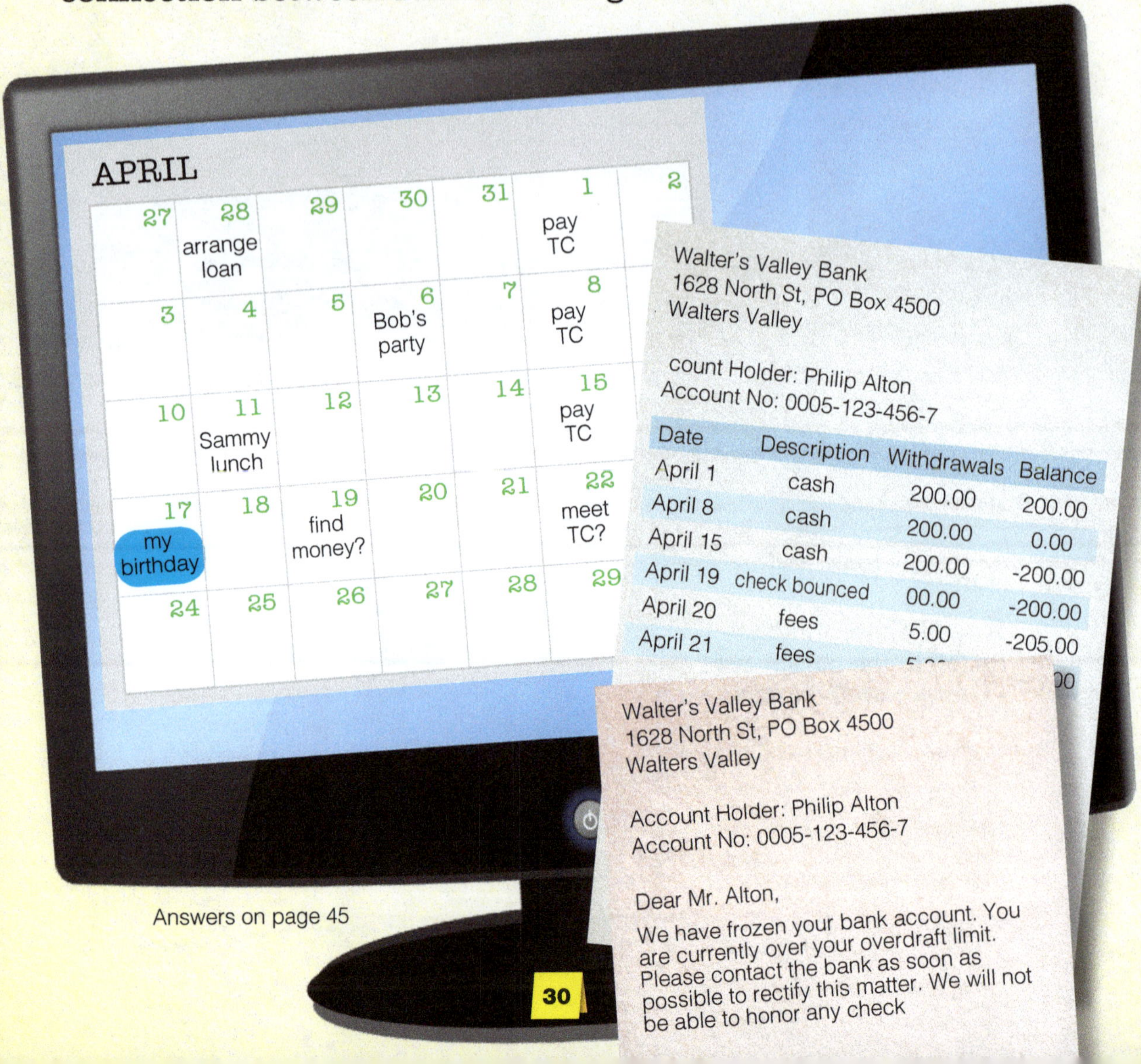

APRIL

27	28 arrange loan	29	30	31	1 pay TC	2
3	4	5	6 Bob's party	7	8 pay TC	
10	11 Sammy lunch	12	13	14	15 pay TC	
17 my birthday	18	19 find money?	20	21	22 meet TC?	
24	25	26	27	28	29	

Walter's Valley Bank
1628 North St, PO Box 4500
Walters Valley

count Holder: Philip Alton
Account No: 0005-123-456-7

Date	Description	Withdrawals	Balance
April 1	cash	200.00	200.00
April 8	cash	200.00	0.00
April 15	cash	200.00	-200.00
April 19	check bounced	00.00	-200.00
April 20	fees	5.00	-205.00
April 21	fees		

Walter's Valley Bank
1628 North St, PO Box 4500
Walters Valley

Account Holder: Philip Alton
Account No: 0005-123-456-7

Dear Mr. Alton,

We have frozen your bank account. You are currently over your overdraft limit. Please contact the bank as soon as possible to rectify this matter. We will not be able to honor any check

Answers on page 45

At first, detectives cannot work out the password to open the victim's phone. His girlfriend Sammy doesn't know it, either. After a little bit of detective work, they manage to get the right numbers. Once they open the phone, they find these text messages between Phil Alton and Tom Cavallaro.

Top Tip

Detectives will usually get a computer specialist to examine cell phones. Otherwise, valuable information can get lost.

Solve It!

Could you have worked out the password and unlocked the victim's phone? The clue will be in his personal files on page 30.

a) the pass code is 1234

b) the pass code is 0417

c) the pass code is 2000

Answers on page 45

Caught on Camera

Detectives have been collecting **CCTV** footage from local businesses and homes in the area near the shooting. CCTV is a very useful tool for the police. More and more streets are being monitored day and night. CCTV **footage** is now often used as a key piece of evidence in court.

Hannah and her team search through hours of footage before they find what they are looking for. They spot an image of the suspect's car racing through a tunnel away from the crime scene.

Top Tip

When a very serious crime has been committed, the police sometimes ask the space agency NASA for satellite photos of an area.

Detectives studying CCTV just sit in a chair, looking at a screen all day. Does that job sound simple to you? It's actually really hard to watch hours of footage and keep concentrating the whole time.

EVIDENCE BAG CHALLENGE

Research shows people can only concentrate fully for 20 to 30 minutes. Imagine doing an 8-hour shift staring at CCTV footage. Would you miss something important?

You will need: a book that you can easily read but has a lot of words and pages, a friend

1. Ask your friend to select an unusual word from your book. It must be the first time the word is used, and be between the middle and the end of the book.
2. Get your friend to tell you the word.
3. Read the book looking for that word. See if you can keep concentrating long enough to find it. Did you manage, or did you get distracted by the story? Or too bored?

If the car on the CCTV isn't stolen, Hannah may be able to link it to the suspect. Usually, cars that are used in crimes have been stolen. Frustratingly, when Hannah traces the car, she finds that it was reported stolen a couple of days before the shooting. All those hours of work have led to a dead end!

SCIENCE DETECTIVE

Remembering a Face

Witnesses are often asked to create a likeness of a suspect. They do this by choosing facial features from a selection presented to them by a special computer program. Can you remember what our suspect Tom Cavallaro looked like? It's not easy to be a witness. Look at the features on these pages and see if you could piece together his likeness.

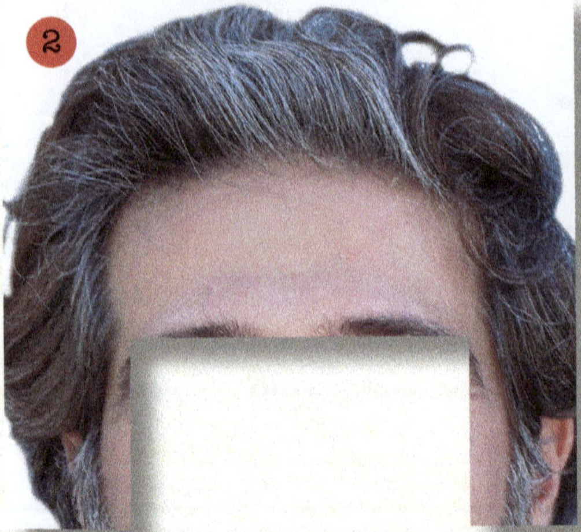

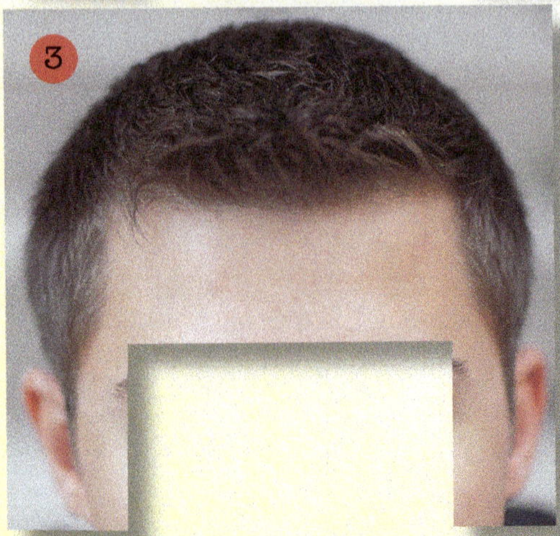

Sometimes, instead of using a computer program, an artist will sketch the criminal from a witness's description. Could you sketch Tom Cavallaro?

Jaws

1
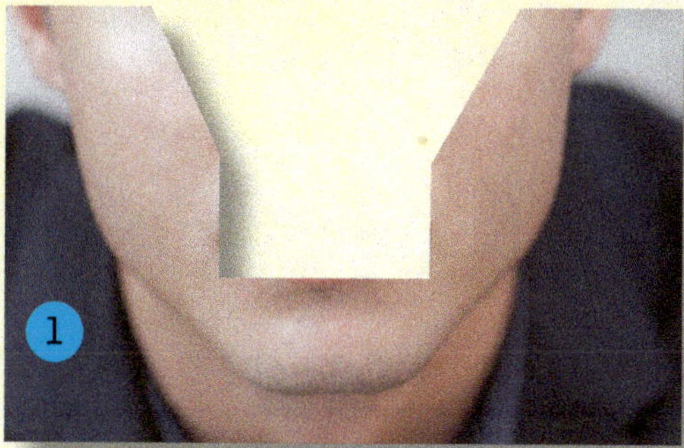

2
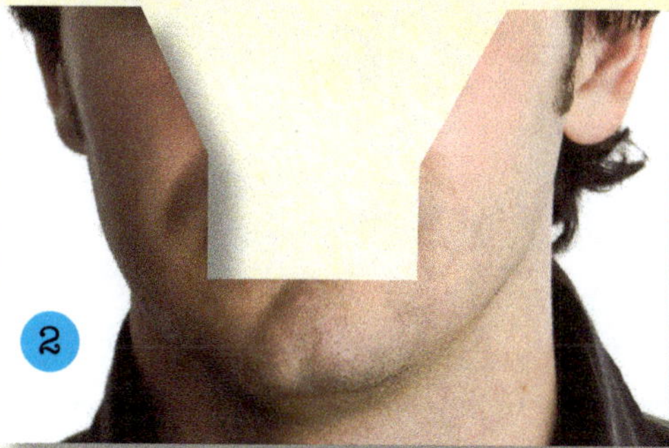

3
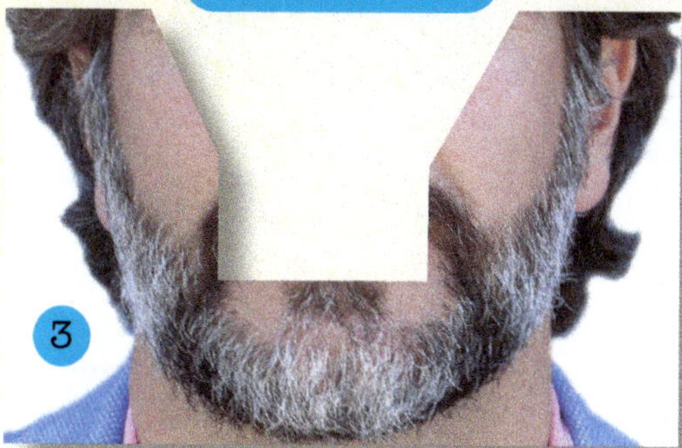

Eyes

1
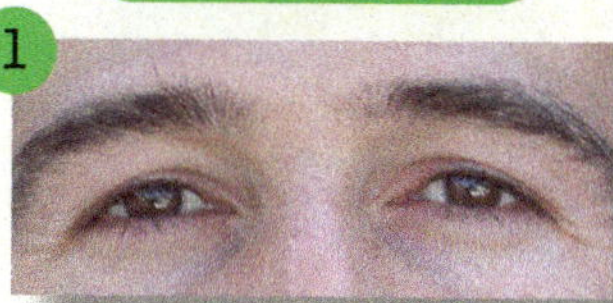

2
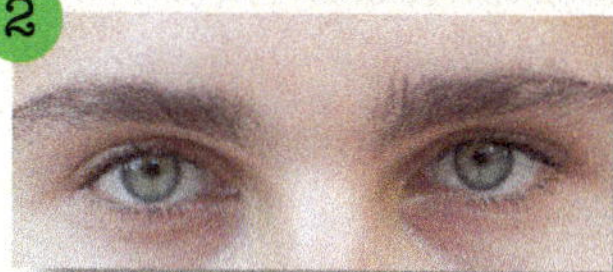

3
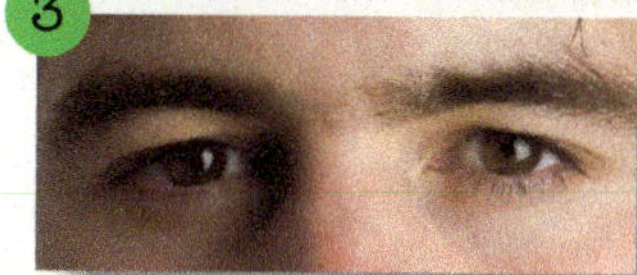

Noses

1
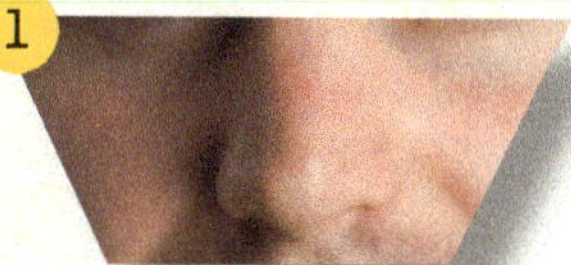

2
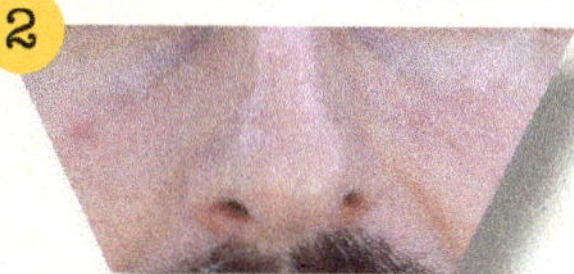

3
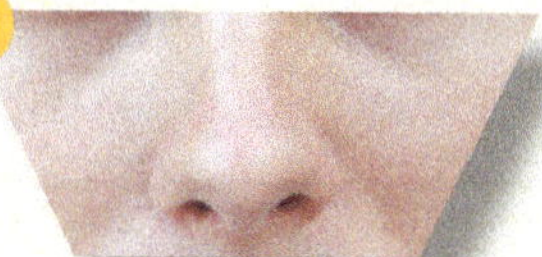

Answers on page 45

Mouths

1
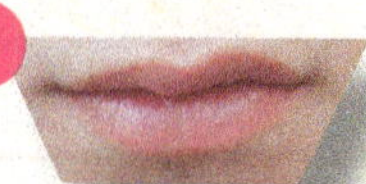

2
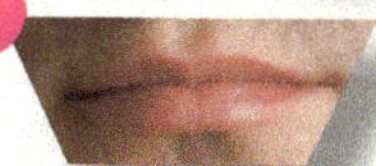

3
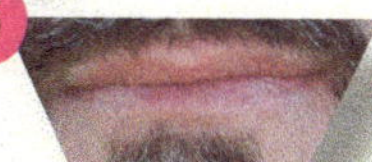

List the different picture categories on a piece of paper. Then write down the number in each category you think is part of Tom Cavallaro's face. Turn to page 29 and see how well you did!

Making an Arrest

Tom Cavallaro is arrested for the shooting. Hannah is not confident that the evidence she has will be enough to convict him, though. Usually police will ask witnesses or victims to identify a suspect in a police line-up. Police gather together members of the public who look a little like the suspect. Witnesses are then asked to look at the line of people and identify who committed the crime. In this case, no one saw the gunman's face. A line-up isn't going to work, but Hannah has another idea...

She remembers the cloth that the gunman used to wipe the gun. There would be other traces on that cloth apart from DNA. She calls in the expert, Rufus the German Shepherd!

Top Tip

A police sniffer dog's amazingly sensitive nose can be used for a scent line-up, instead!

A special machine is used to suck up smells from the cloth onto a scent pad. Detective Rufus sniffs the scent pad, walks along the line of people, and sits next to Tom Cavallaro! Hannah has a positive identification at last!

Solve It!

Proving a suspect committed a crime with evidence is key to sending a criminal to jail. Detectives also want to find a motive. A motive is a reason why someone does something. What do you think our gunman's motive might be?

a) Tom Cavallaro was angry that his brother was in jail

b) Phil Alton owed Tom Cavallaro money

c) Tom Cavallaro's gang made Tom shoot Phil Alton

Answers on page 45

SCIENCE DETECTIVE

Following the Footsteps

On the way to his jail cell, Cavallaro suddenly breaks loose and makes a run for it. He doesn't get very far! Workers are painting the woodwork outside the police station. Cavallaro knocks a paint can over as he is running away, and his shoes get covered in paint. Detectives follow his footprints and easily find his hiding place!

Top Tip

Detective work can be easier in winter. When someone reports a crime, the criminal can sometimes escape before police get there. This may not matter after a snowfall. Why? Police can see where the criminal went by tracking their footprints in the snow!

Tracking Footprints

A footprint left behind at a crime scene can lead detectives to the criminal in another way, too. Shoes can leave distinctive prints which can help to identify suspects. If its sole is worn or marked, a shoe-print can be almost as unique as a fingerprint.

Can you match this set of prints to one of the sets below?

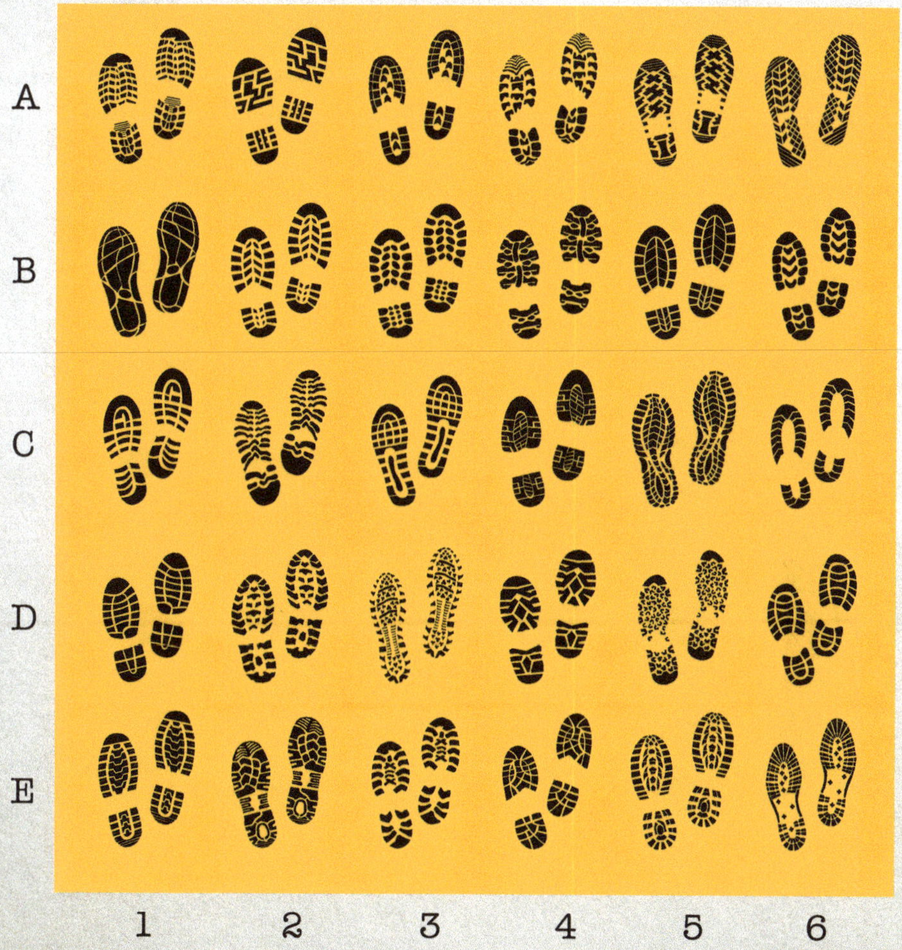

Answers on page 45

A Secret Message

Hannah needs to prepare her evidence before Cavallaro's trial. She has a motive for the shooting, but she could use some proof that Tom Cavallaro threatened Phil Alton.

She goes to meet one of her **informants**, Harvey. Informants are people, usually criminals, hired by detectives to give them inside information. The police keep the informant's identity secret to protect them. A criminal gang like the Cavallaros would not be too pleased to know someone was giving away information about them to the police!

Having an inside man in the gang proved useful. Harvey had some great information. He told Hannah that Tom Cavallaro would write threatening notes to anyone who owed them money. His notepad may have an impression of the last note he wrote. Hannah's team had searched Tom Cavallaro's apartment. His notepad might be in the police evidence locker!

EVIDENCE BAG CHALLENGE

Leave a secret note for a friend to find. Try this challenge.

You will need: a notepad, a ballpoint pen, a soft-leaded pencil.

1. Ask your friend to write a secret message on the notepad using the ballpoint pen. Tell them to press hard as they write.
2. Get your friend to then rip off the sheet of paper they wrote on and put it in their pocket.
3. Using the side of the pencil lead, gently draw all over the new top sheet of paper on the notepad. You should see the secret message magically appear!

The pencil will color all of the paper except the area that was pressed in by the ballpoint pen.

The Verdict

Hannah is happy now that she has more evidence. The note found at Tom Cavallaro's apartment will help her case. She prepares all her evidence to present in court. It doesn't matter how many times she has been to court, it still makes her feel nervous. By the time the trial happens, it is many months after she investigated the case. She reads back through all her notes, to make sure her evidence is perfect.

Solve It!

Luckily, Phil Alton recovers and marries his girlfriend, Sammy. He comes to court to give evidence against Tom Cavallaro. The police know that even if Tom is sent to prison, the Cavallaro gang may try to get revenge on Mr. Alton. What can the police do to protect him?

a) He will be looked after for the rest of his life by a witness protection program.

b) He and his new wife will be given a new name and identity and be moved to a new area.

c) They will be given money until he has found a new job.

d) All of the above

Answers on page 45

The Accused

Name: Tom Cavallaro

Date of Trial: 05/19/2018
Court No: Court One

Judge Presiding: P.T. Patterson

Crime: Aggravated Assault with a Deadly Weapon

Profile: Tom Cavallaro was a member of the Cavallaro gang. He had been accused of a robbery, along with his brother Harry, in 2014. There was not enough evidence to send him to jail that time. He was thought to have been involved in a number of crimes, but no one was brave enough to give evidence against him. He had a reputation for getting revenge on anyone who crossed him.

The jury must decide whether Tom Cavallaro is guilty or innocent. Because of the reputation of the Cavallaro gang, the police give the members of the jury all personal protection during the trial, too! Now it's up to them to decide. What do you think?

GUILTY or **NOT GUILTY**

Glossary

alibi Proof that a person accused of a crime was at another place when the crime occurred.

angle The figure formed by two lines extending from the same point.

ballistic Dealing with the motion of objects (as bullets or rockets) that are thrown or driven forward.

CCTV Closed-circuit television.

confess To admit to having done something wrong.

crime scene The place where an offense has been committed and forensic evidence may be gathered.

databases Collections of data that are organized especially to be used by a computer.

deflated Not inflated.

dispatched To send away quickly to a particular place or for a particular purpose.

DNA The code in each person's cells that makes everyone unique.

drive-by A crime that occurs from a moving vehicle.

evidence Material presented to a court in a crime case.

footage Film recording an event.

genes A part of DNA that contains chemical information controlling or influencing an inherited trait such as eye color.

hesitate To stop or pause because of uncertainty or indecision.

informants People who give information about someone else.

inherited Received money or property from a person after their death.

innocent Free from guilt or blame.

insured Protected by a contract by which someone guarantees to pay someone else a specified amount after the person's injury or death.

jury A group of people in court who must decide whether someone is guilty or not.

kidnapped To carry away a person by unlawful force or by fraud and against his or her will.

logical according to the rules of sound reasoning.

partial Not total or complete.

reasoning To use the power of reason.

suspect A person believed to have committed a crime.

velocity Speed.

witnesses One present at an action such as a crime who can testify to its having taken place.

Answers

page 5 - c, page 6 - c, page 9 - a, page 13 - a, page 17 - the medal that was hanging on the radiator, page 18 - b, page 25 - b, page 29 - c, page 30 - "TC" in the diary might be Tom Cavallaro, page 31 - b, page 34-35 - hair = 2, jaw = 3, eyes = 1, nose = 2, mouth = 3, page 37 - b, page 39 - row D, column 3, page 42 - d

Want to Be a Detective?

Job: Detective

Job Description: Police detectives interview suspects, witnesses, and victims to piece together the crime that they are investigating. Detectives work closely with crime scene investigators, who gather forensic evidence police detectives need to work their cases. They may have to testify in court. Police detectives do everything they can to get justice for the victim while keeping them and their family up-to-date with the progress of their case.

Qualifications needed: Most detectives have a bachelor's degree in criminal justice. To become a detective, they first serve as a police officer for a period of time, generally 1 to 5 years. They will usually complete further training, preferably at a master's degree level.

Employment: General detectives do general investigation. Others specialize in certain types of crime. Homicide detectives focus on suspicious deaths. Others may specialize in financial crimes or drug-related crimes. A detective's time is mostly spent investigating or doing paperwork. They are expected to stay physically fit.

Career Advice

Further Information

Books

Gardner, Robert. *Crime Lab 101: 25 Different Experiments in Crime Detection.* Mineola, NY: Dover Publications, 2013.

Waddell, Dan. *How To Be a Detective.* Somerville, MA: Candlewick Press, 2012.

Websites

A website with two cool detective project ideas
http://lifestyle.howstuffworks.com/crafts/seasonal/winter/detective-activities-for-kids.htm

Lots of crimes to solve on this Mysterynet website
http://kids.mysterynet.com/solveit/

Index